TURNING POINTS IN
SEPTEMBER 11"
ATTACKS

by Christopher Forest

pogo

Ideas for Parents and Teachers

Pogo Books let children practice reading informational text while introducing them to nonfiction features such as headings, labels, sidebars, maps, and diagrams, as well as a table of contents, glossary, and index.

Carefully leveled text with a strong photo match offers early fluent readers the support they need to succeed.

Before Reading

- "Walk" through the book and point out the various nonfiction features. Ask the student what purpose each feature serves.
- Look at the glossary together. Read and discuss the words.

Read the Book

- Have the child read the book independently.
- Invite him or her to list questions that arise from reading.

After Reading

- Discuss the child's questions. Talk about how he or she might find answers to those questions.
- Prompt the child to think more. Ask: What did you know about the September 11th attacks before reading this book? What more would you like to know?

Pogo Books are published by Jump!
5357 Penn Avenue South
Minneapolis, MN 55419
www.jumplibrary.com

Copyright © 2021 Jump!
International copyright reserved in all countries.
No part of this book may be reproduced in any form without written permission from the publisher.

Library of Congress Cataloging-in-Publication Data

Names: Forest, Christopher, author.
Title: September 11th attacks / Christopher Forest.
Description: Minneapolis: Jump!, Inc., 2021.
Series: Turning points in U.S. history
Includes index.
Audience: Ages 7–10. | Audience: Grades 2–3.
Identifiers: LCCN 2019049917 (print)
LCCN 2019049918 (ebook)
ISBN 9781645274407 (hardcover)
ISBN 9781645274414 (paperback)
ISBN 9781645274421 (ebook)
Subjects: LCSH: September 11 Terrorist Attacks, 2001–Juvenile literature. | Terrorism–Juvenile literature. Qaida (Organization)–Juvenile literature.
Classification: LCC HV6432.7.F666 2021 (print)
LCC HV6432.7 (ebook)
DDC 973.931–dc23
LC record available at https://lccn.loc.gov/2019049917
LC ebook record available at https://lccn.loc.gov/2019049918

Editor: Jenna Gleisner
Designer: Jenna Casura

Photo Credits: Bob London/Alamy, cover; Everett Collection Inc/Alamy, 1; CBW/Alamy, 3; Historic Collection/Alamy, 4; Chao Soi Cheong/AP Images, 5; Spencer Platt/Getty, 6–7; New York Daily News Archive/Getty, 8; John Moore/Getty, 9; Richard Levine/Alamy, 10–11; Archive Image/Alamy, 12–13; Everett Collection Historical/Alamy, 14–15; White House Photo/Alamy, 16; Jim Lambert/Shutterstock, 17; PJF Military Collection/Alamy, 18–19; LeoPatrizi/iStock, 20–21; dibrova/Shutterstock, 23.

Printed in the United States of America at Corporate Graphics in North Mankato, Minnesota.

TABLE OF CONTENTS

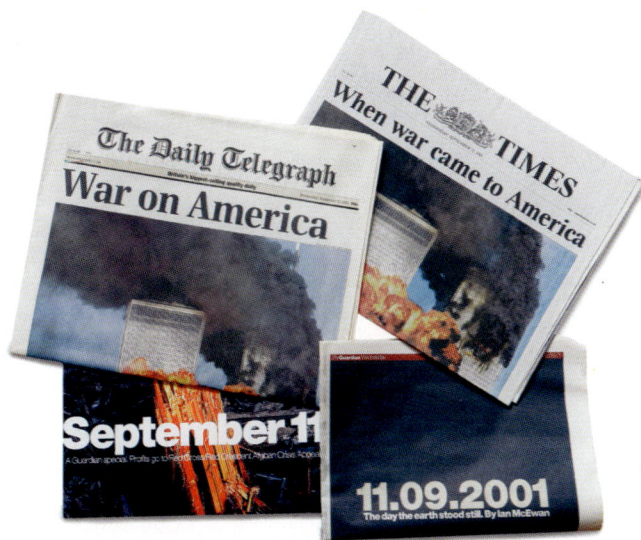

CHAPTER 1

TWIN TOWERS ATTACKED

The morning of September 11, 2001, seemed normal to the people in New York City. It was a sunny day. Many people went to work.

twin towers

That changed at exactly 8:46 a.m. An airplane crashed into the World Trade Center. Many people worked there. It had two towers. They were called the twin towers. The airplane hit the north tower.

It looked like a horrible accident. But 17 minutes later, people knew it was not. Why? Another airplane struck the south tower. It became clear. The United States was under attack.

WHAT DO YOU THINK?

How do you think people felt when the airplane hit the south tower? How would you have felt?

?

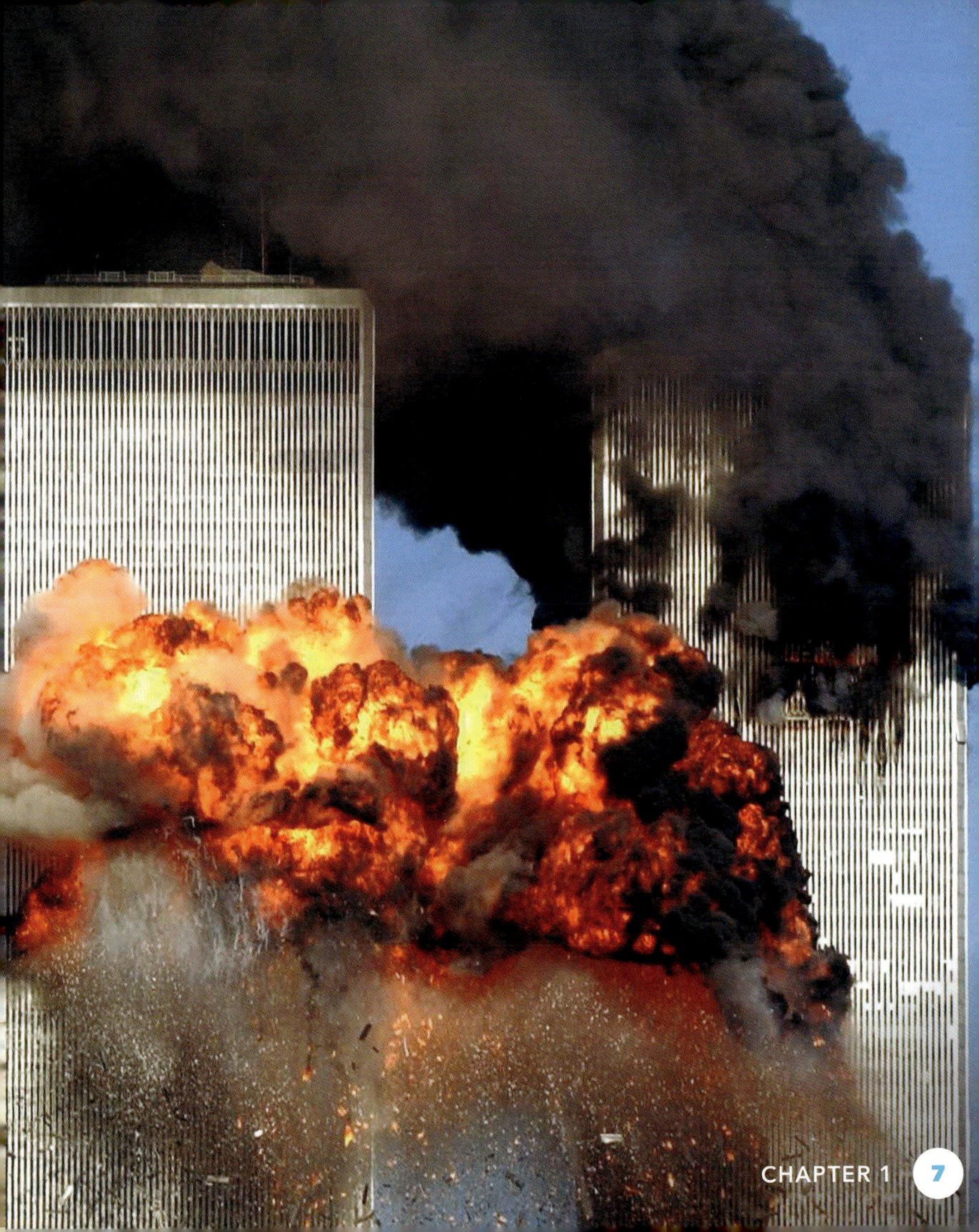

CHAPTER 2

FOUR AIRPLANES

The attackers were part of a **terrorist** group. It is called al-Qaeda. This group formed in 1988. Osama bin Laden was their leader.

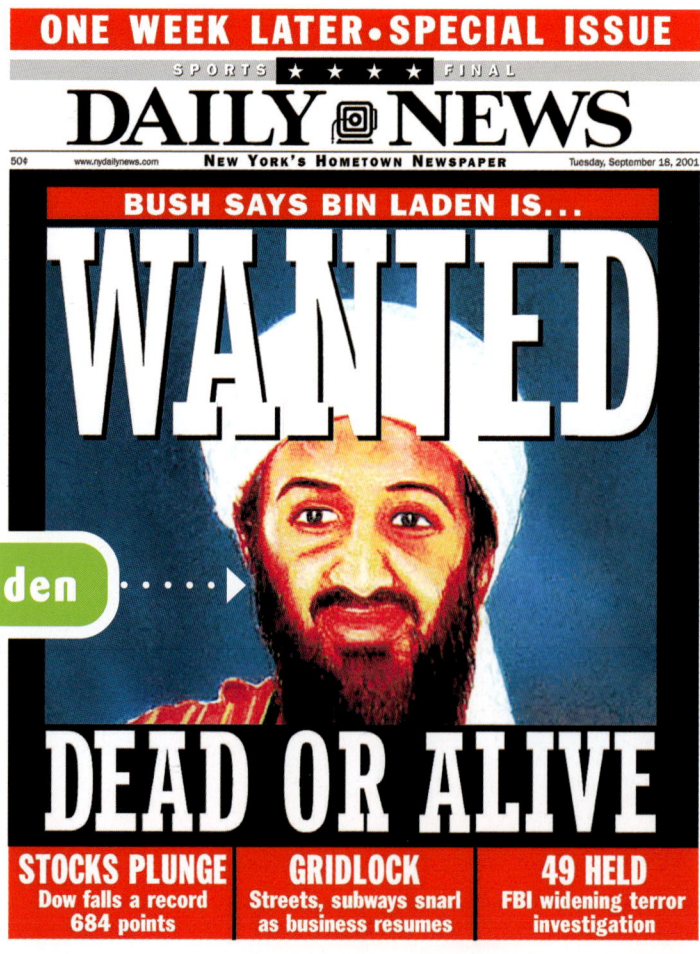

Osama bin Laden

ONE WEEK LATER·SPECIAL ISSUE

SPORTS ★★★★★ FINAL

DAILY NEWS

50¢ www.nydailynews.com NEW YORK'S HOMETOWN NEWSPAPER Tuesday, September 18, 2001

BUSH SAYS BIN LADEN IS...

WANTED

DEAD OR ALIVE

STOCKS PLUNGE
Dow falls a record 684 points

GRIDLOCK
Streets, subways snarl as business resumes

49 HELD
FBI widening terror investigation

U.S. soldiers

Al-Qaeda disagreed with American ideas. U.S. soldiers were in the **Middle East**. Al-Qaeda did not want them there. They were angry with the United States. They wanted to show power.

first responders

On September 11, 2001, 19 men from al-Qaeda **hijacked** four airplanes. Two airplanes struck the twin towers. People rushed out of the towers. The towers **collapsed**. Thousands survived. But more than 2,600 people died. Thousands more were hurt.

WHAT DO YOU THINK?

First responders rushed to the scene of the attack. Many were firefighters and police. They risked their lives to help people. Why do you think they did this?

A third airplane struck the Pentagon. This is a **military** building in Virginia. The crash caused 189 deaths.

A fourth airplane was also hijacked. Its passengers heard about the other airplanes. They fought the hijackers. They tried to take back control of the airplane. It crashed in Shanksville, Pennsylvania. There were 40 **victims**.

DID YOU KNOW?

Where were the hijackers taking the fourth airplane? No one knows for sure. Many think it was Washington, D.C. Some think they were going to the U.S. Capitol Building. Others believe they were going to the White House.

Pentagon

In total, 2,996 people died in the September 11th attacks. Thousands more were injured. Buildings were destroyed.

TAKE A LOOK!

What were the routes of the airplanes on September 11, 2001? Take a look.

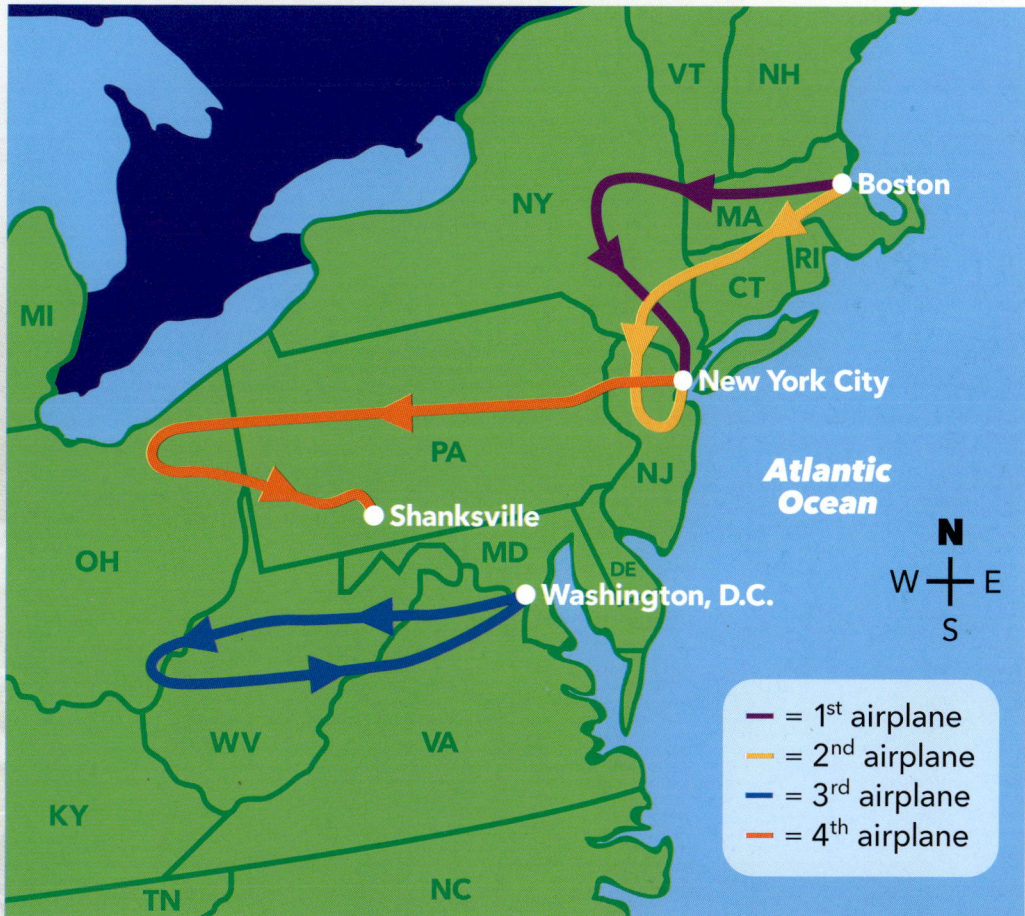

VT NH

NY MA RI
CT

Boston

MI

New York City

PA

NJ

Atlantic Ocean

Shanksville

OH MD

DE

Washington, D.C.

N
W   E
S

WV VA

KY

— = 1st airplane
— = 2nd airplane
— = 3rd airplane
— = 4th airplane

TN NC

CHAPTER 3

AFTER THE ATTACKS

The attacks changed the United States. How? President George W. Bush declared war. He called it the War on Terror. The U.S. military fought many terrorists. Ten years later, U.S. soldiers found and killed bin Laden.

President George W. Bush ......▶

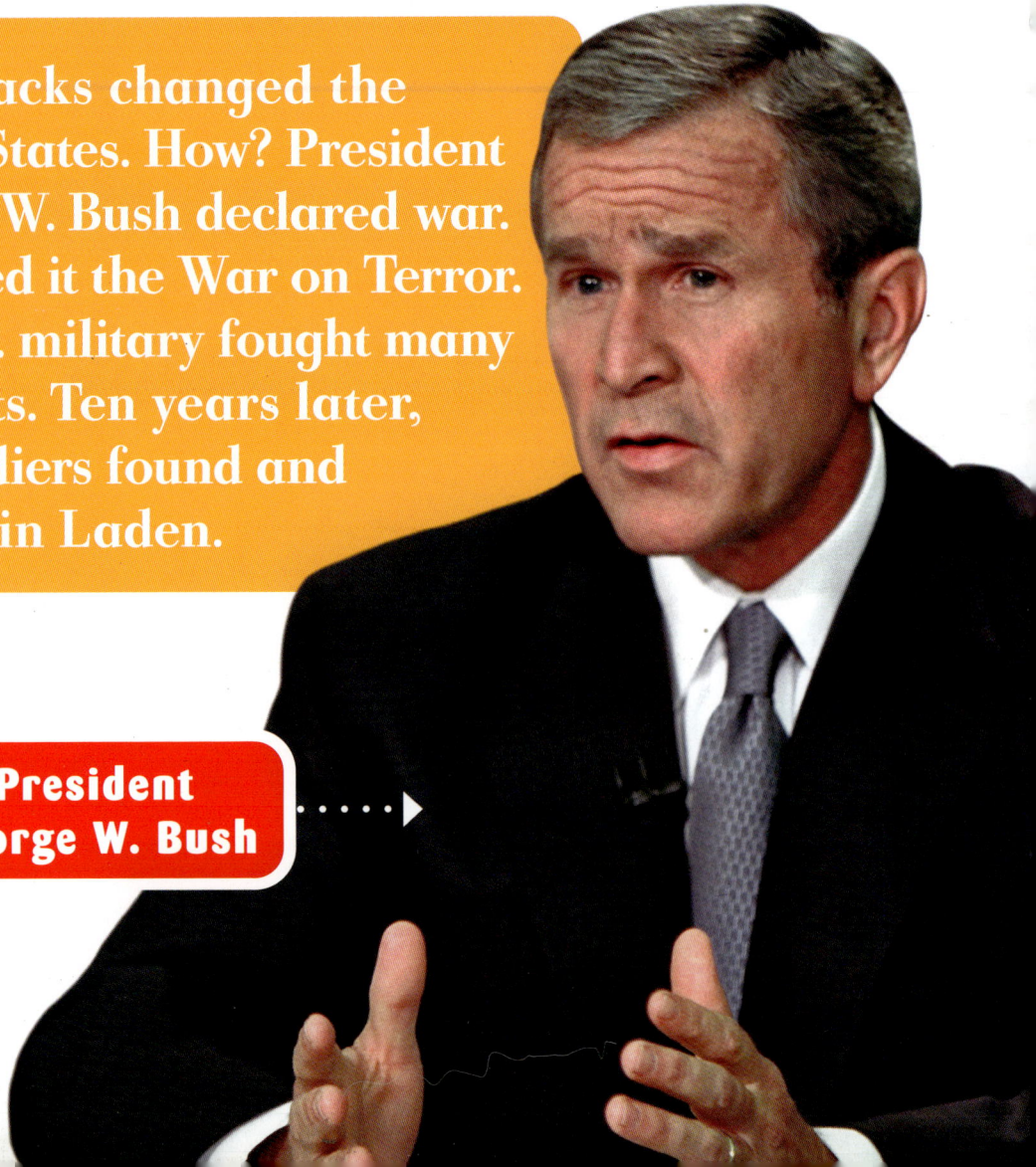

The Department of Homeland Security was formed. It protects Americans from terrorists. It made new safety rules. Some are still used in airports. Many are used at public buildings, too.

airport security

Notice of Additional Screening

Carry on bags waiting for additional screening
DO NOT REMOVE

STOP

Your safety is our priority

Americans showed more **patriotism** after the attacks. They hung flags. They remembered the events of that day.

Now it is remembered each year. Patriot Day honors those affected by the attacks. People hold ceremonies.

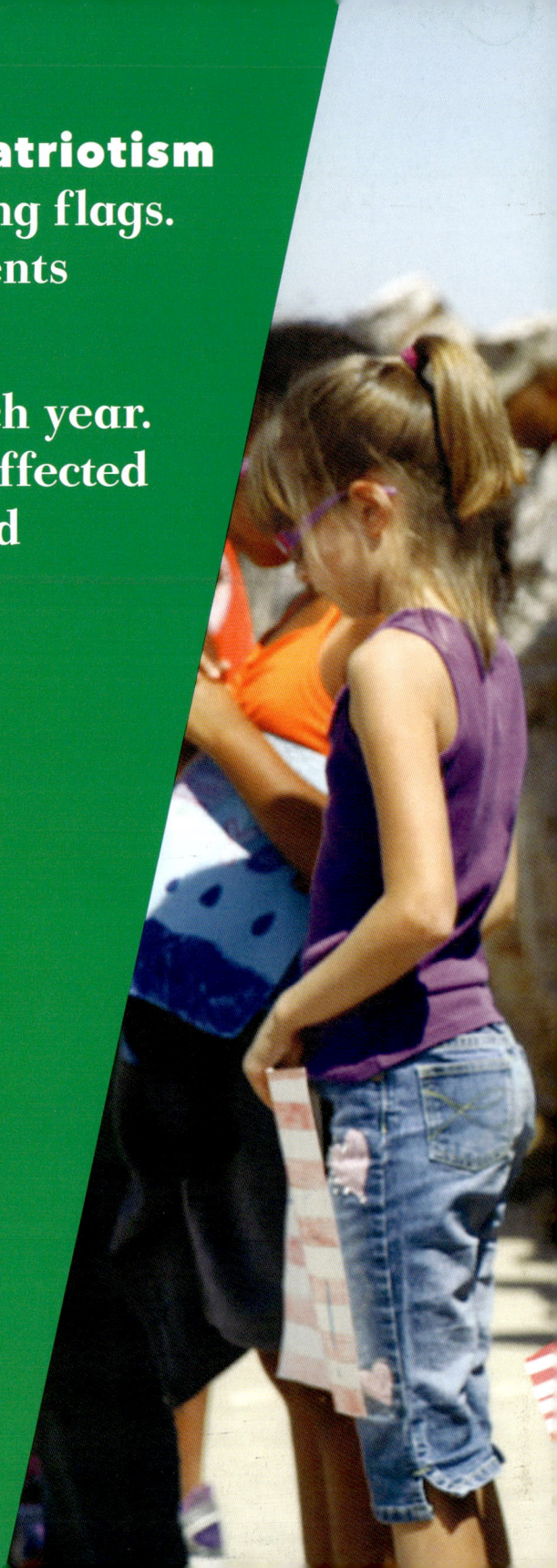

museum

reflecting pool

A **memorial** was built. It opened in 2012. It includes a museum and two pools. The pools sit where the twin towers used to be.

These attacks changed the country forever. U.S. soldiers fought terrorists. Security tightened. We remember. We honor the victims of the September 11th attacks.

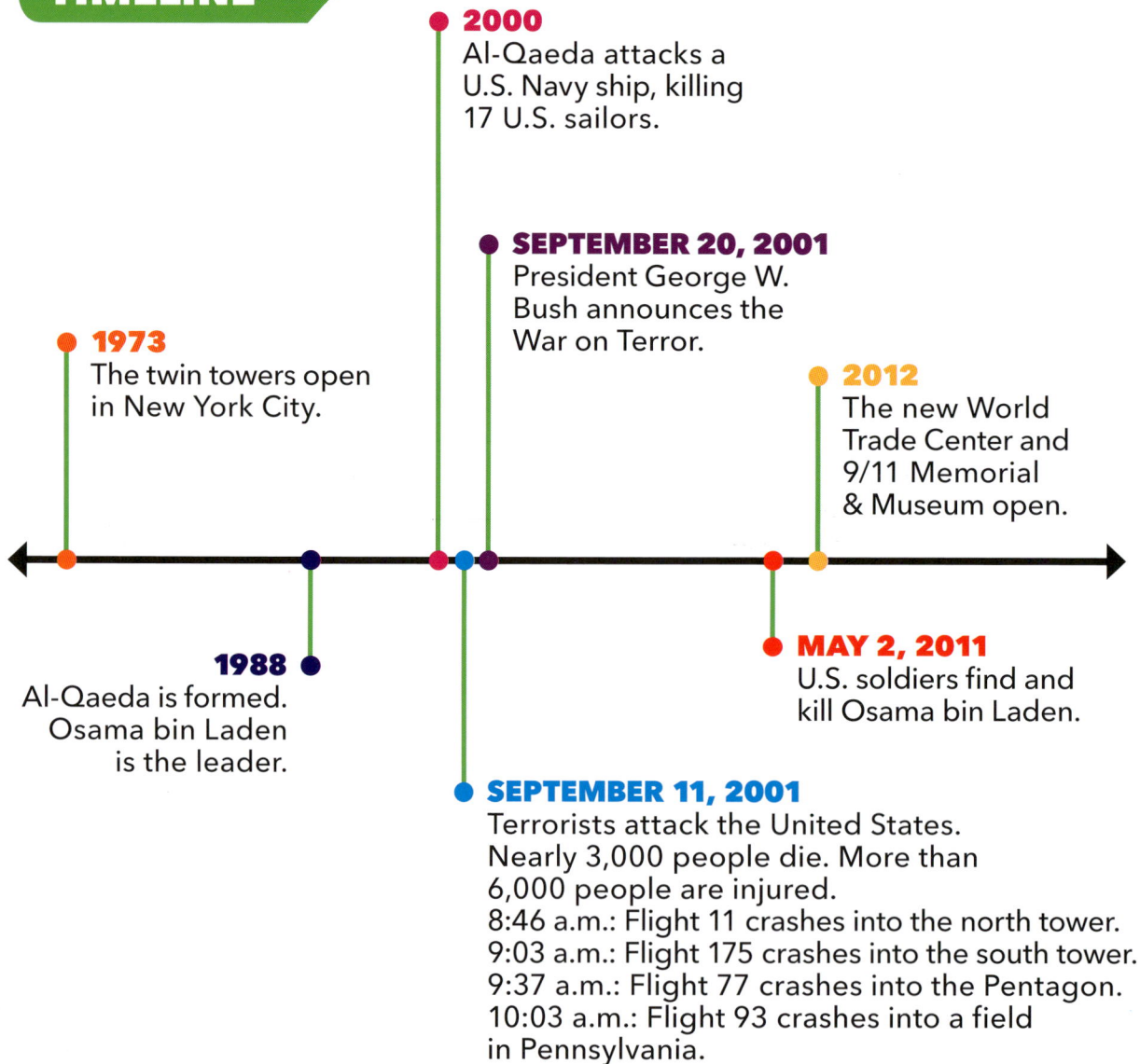

QUICK FACTS & TOOLS

TIMELINE

1973
The twin towers open in New York City.

1988
Al-Qaeda is formed. Osama bin Laden is the leader.

2000
Al-Qaeda attacks a U.S. Navy ship, killing 17 U.S. sailors.

SEPTEMBER 11, 2001
Terrorists attack the United States. Nearly 3,000 people die. More than 6,000 people are injured.
8:46 a.m.: Flight 11 crashes into the north tower.
9:03 a.m.: Flight 175 crashes into the south tower.
9:37 a.m.: Flight 77 crashes into the Pentagon.
10:03 a.m.: Flight 93 crashes into a field in Pennsylvania.

SEPTEMBER 20, 2001
President George W. Bush announces the War on Terror.

MAY 2, 2011
U.S. soldiers find and kill Osama bin Laden.

2012
The new World Trade Center and 9/11 Memorial & Museum open.

GLOSSARY

collapsed: Fell suddenly and completely.

first responders: People, such as police officers, firefighters, and paramedics, whose job is to respond first in an emergency.

hijacked: Took control of a vehicle and forced it to go somewhere.

memorial: Something that is built, such as a statue or monument, to help people remember a person or event.

Middle East: A region that is made up of parts of Africa and Asia and includes countries such as Egypt, Iran, Iraq, Israel, Saudi Arabia, Syria, and Turkey.

military: Of or having to do with soldiers, the armed forces, or war.

patriotism: Showing a strong loyalty to one's country.

terrorist: A person who uses violence and threats to frighten people, obtain power, or force a government to do something.

victims: People who are injured or killed.

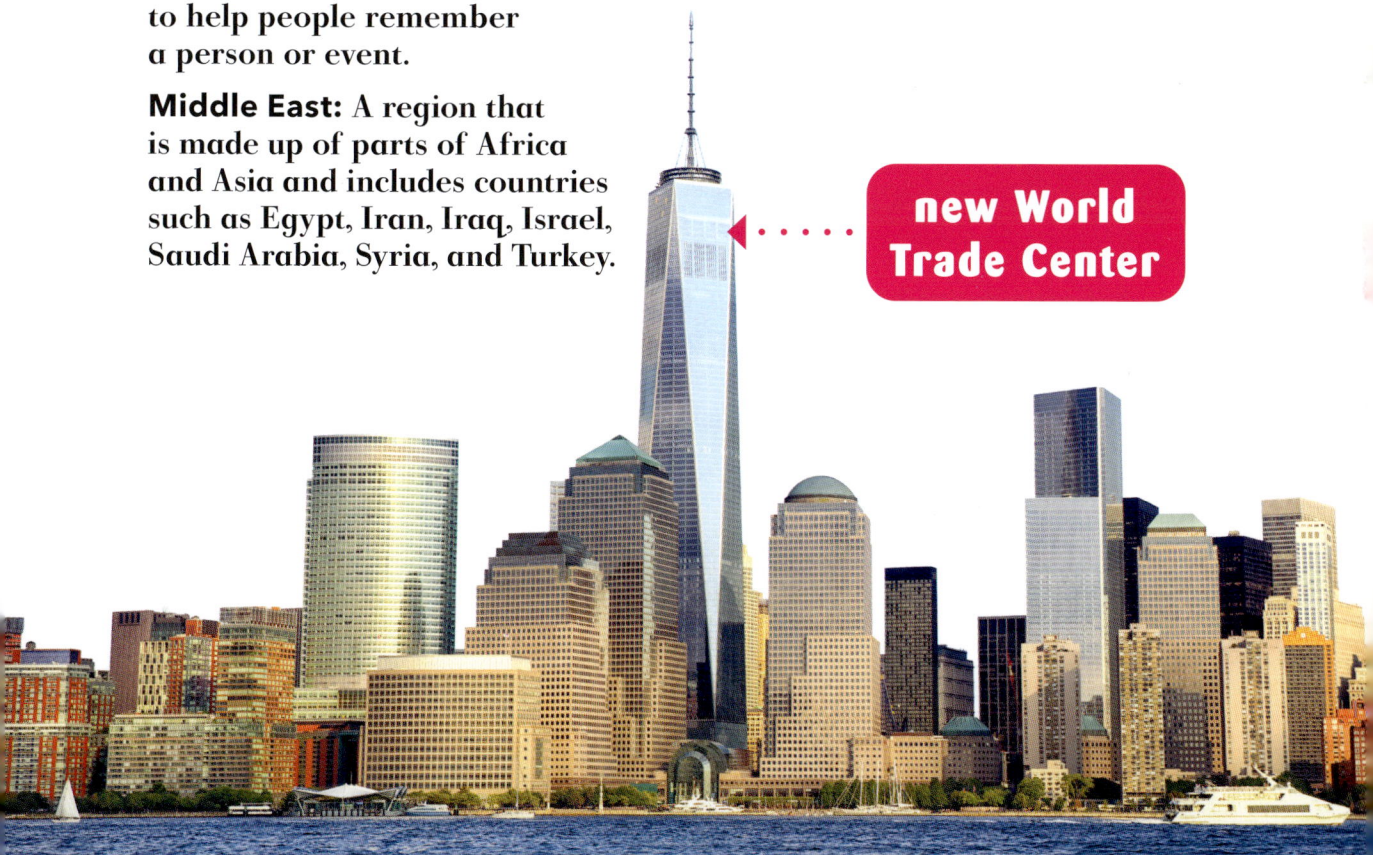

new World Trade Center

INDEX

TO LEARN MORE

Finding more information is as easy as 1, 2, 3.

❶ Go to www.factsurfer.com

❷ Enter "September11thattacks" into the search box.

❸ Choose your book to see a list of websites.

FACT SURFER